TIMEVIEW

DOCTOR WHO

TIMEVIEW

FRANK BELLAMY

THE DOCTOR WHO ILLUSTRATIONS

By arrangement with the British Broadcasting Corporation

COMMENTARY BY DAVID BELLAMY

Who Dares Publishing

CONTENTS

Phototypeset, Printed and Bound in Great Britain
by Burgess & Son (Abingdon) Ltd. for the Publisher,
Who Dares Publishing, 3 Durrant Road,
Bournemouth, Dorset BH2 6NE

Designed by Cherriwyn Magill

First Printing 1985
ISBN 0 948487 03 8 TPB
ISBN 0 948487 02 X HARDCOVER

Special thanks to Jeremy Bentham, Brian Thomas,
David Driver, Wallace Grevatt and Robert Davis.

Photograph of Frank Bellamy used by kind permission
of the Northamptonshire Evening Telegraph.

David Bellamy is a graphic designer and lives
in Kettering, Northamptonshire.

The *Radio Times* is a weekly magazine giving details of the BBC radio and television programmes and is published by BBC Publications. It has traditionally been known for the high standard of commissioned illustrations. It was first published in 1923 and still flourishes today with an average weekly circulation in excess of three million.

Frank Bellamy was born in Kettering, Northants in 1917 and after being demobbed from the army at the end of the war returned to work in a Kettering art studio. To fulfil a lifelong ambition he landed a job in a Fleet Street art studio two years later, despite his lack of formal training. In 1953 he went freelance and his long, creative relationship with the picture strip began, establishing his style and reputation through a variety of remarkable full colour strips for the famous *Eagle* comic, for which he worked from 1957 until 1966. Later work included some truly outstanding graphic artwork for *TV21*, a quality comic based around Gerry Anderson's television creations, illustrations for the *Radio Times, Sunday Times Magazine* and even a collaboration with television for one of *The Avengers* episodes, 'The Winged Avenger'. In 1971 he took over the long-running 'Garth' strip in the *Daily Mirror*. He was a Fellow of the Society of Industrial Artists and in 1972 received 'Best Foreign Artist' award from the American Academy of Comic Book Arts. He died in 1976, remembered as a true original with a secured world-wide reputation as one of the greatest dramatic illustrators we have seen.

INTRODUCTION

Frank Bellamy and *Doctor Who* were a unique combination that began in 1971 when David Driver, then Art Editor of the *Radio Times* commissioned him to illustrate a two and a half page picture strip to accompany a feature on the Time Lord. His bold dramatic style was ideal for portraying the adventures of the Doctor and this was to be the start of a long running series of *Doctor Who* artwork he completed for the magazine, his last contribution being made in 1976. Many of the illustrations were reproduced little more than postage stamp size and as Bellamy always preferred to draw as close to same size as possible, it is extraordinary that he was able to produce worthwhile cameos with this restriction imposed upon him.

It is commonly believed that Bellamy, in addition to a number of individual montages, illustrated the entire ninth, tenth and eleventh seasons of the *Doctor Who* programmes. In fact some occasional drawings for the ninth and tenth seasons and the entire eleventh season were the work of other illustrators in 'the style of' Bellamy who was himself unavailable at that time.

Frank Bellamy also completed three full colour feature illustrations and a full colour cover, 'The Day of the Daleks' which was the first of only two *Doctor Who* artwork covers for the *Radio Times*, the other being for 'The Five Doctors' by Andrew Skilleter in 1983.

Frank Bellamy was a remarkable illustrator, a true original, respected by fellow professionals in the United Kingdom, United States and elsewhere in the world, and admired by many who avidly followed his work. This book, which reprints for the first time the complete collection of his Doctor Who work, represents just a fraction of his output. The work would never have existed but for the traditional creative policy of the *Radio Times* and equally this book would have been impossible without their generous co-operation, and in particular that of its Deputy and Art Editor, Brian Thomas, who dealt personally with

Bellamy during those years and has a great respect for his work. He recalls when he was Assistant Art Editor of Programme Pages, Frank Bellamy's Morden house was on his route home and he would occasionally drop in the scripts and photographic reference for *Doctor Who* on a Friday evening. A commission for the *Radio Times* was, and still is, usually a weekend affair.

The work has been reproduced by necessity from the printed pages of the *Radio Times*, despite a concerted search for the original artwork from which ideally we would have preferred to reproduce. Only the piece of Tom Baker and the Loch Ness Monster is from the original artwork. Every effort has been made, however, to ensure the best quality reproduction possible and the graphic power of his illustrations still comes across as strong as the day they were first printed.

We are delighted to have David Bellamy writing a commentary to this book, revealing for the first time intimate insights into the life and work of his father. From his unique position he has been able to recall discussions and observations of this extraordinary artist at work.

Welcome then to this view of time ...

THE DAEMONS

A superstition surrounding the ancient barrow at Devil's End comes true when a strange force kills an archaeologist. The Master has called up the Daemon, Azal, the force of which has isolated the village.

Originally from outer space, the Daemons were prehistoric settlers on Earth. Azal is the only one who remains. He will bestow the benefit of his power on a Human who can put it to good use, or will ensure the destruction of the planet!

The Doctor manages to make an escape, but the villagers, who are being manipulated by the Master, attack him. When Azal offers to grant him his power he rejects it. Jo intervenes to save the Doctor from being killed and, bewildered by her courage, Azal annihilates himself. The Master is taken prisoner.

My father's whole life concentrated on art and I believe his
very exciting graphic style was partly due to being a rather
shy and reserved person – those very vibrant and powerful
illustrations were a form of self expression for him.

Although he personally had a wonderful sense of humour he took his work extremely seriously, believing that if he worked in that way he would convey his style with the most impact, which of course he did. He disliked the use of the word 'comic' strip – it was always 'picture' strip or 'continuation' strip to him, and he was always most anxious to distance himself from the misconceived idea of most people that a 'comic strip' was something rather humorous.

THE CURSE OF PELADON

The King of Peladon and Torbis, his Chancellor, wish their planet to join the Galactic Federation. Hepesh, the High Priest, is against the proposal. But when Torbis is killed, the finger of suspicion falls on the magical beast Aggedor.

Alpha Centauri, Arcturus and the Ice Warrior, Izlyr, are sent to Peladon by the Federation. When the Doctor and Jo are despatched there by the Time Lords, the Doctor is mistaken for the adviser from Earth. He discovers that Hepesh and Arcturus are responsible for the death of Torbis, and the Ice Warriors help him to unmask the culprits. Hepesh commands Aggedor to slay the King, but the monster obeys the Doctor and Hepesh is killed.

The real committee member from Earth then arrives, and the Doctor departs.

COLONY IN SPACE

The Time Lords send the Doctor and Jo into the mid twenty-first century. The TARDIS transports them to a dismal planet where the Master is plotting to steal the Doomsday Machine. Heavily guarded, this machine is so powerful that even its inventors have fallen under its spell, now living as Primitives.

Also inhabiting the planet are Colonists who have emigrated from Earth. They are attempting against all the odds to form a farming community, while the rival Interplanetary Mining Corporation are planning to extract valuable mineral resources. The Master presents himself as the expert sent to consider the situation.

The Doctor and Jo help the Colonists, then foil the Master's plot. They persuade the priest guardian, and only member of his race left, to programme the Doomsday Machine to destroy itself.

DOCTOR WHO in colony in SPACE

In his last adventure 'Vampire from Space,' Dr Who used his space/time machine the Tardis to save Earth from the alien parasite creature Axos by forcing it into a time-loop. But Dr Who is afraid that the Master, who sent Axos to destroy Earth, has escaped and will fight again . . . now read on

FRANK BELLAMY

I'VE DONE IT! I'VE MADE A NEW DEMATERIALISATION CIRCUIT FOR THE TARDIS!

BUT WILL IT WORK? THE TIME LORDS MEAN TO KEEP ME HERE ON EARTH...

MEANWHILE SOMEWHERE IN SPACE AND TIME...

THE REPORT ON THE DOOMSDAY WEAPON IS MISSING. THE MASTER MUST HAVE TAKEN IT!

WHY NOT USE THE DOCTOR TO DEAL WITH HIM? BUT WAIT—

WE'VE IMMOBILISED HIS TARDIS.

THEN LET US RESTORE HIS FREEDOM — FOR AS LONG AS IT SERVES OUR PURPOSE...

... AND BACK ON EARTH.

NOW WE'LL TRY OUT THE NEW CIRCUIT.

DOCTOR! THE DOORS HAVE CLOSED!

All his life he was particularly interested in films and when he first started work at a local studio in Kettering in the 1930s he designed film posters for the popular gangster movies of that era. The main highlight of the week was going to his cinema and seeing these exciting images appear on the screen. I am convinced he was influenced by the use of the close-up and the various action sequences of his particular favourites, the Humphrey Bogart, James Cagney gangster movies. They were rather dimly lit and atmospheric and I particularly remember he said he liked his work to convey more than anything else a sense of atmosphere. Through a very clever use of lighting he was

20

THE SEA DEVILS

The Master is in prison on an island. Trenchard informs the Doctor and Jo that some ships are missing but while trying to find out the facts, the Doctor is set upon by a Sea Devil, a human-like reptile.

A plot uncovered by the Doctor reveals that Trenchard is helping the Master steal components from a naval base. The Master is constructing a machine to control the world by putting the Sea Devils in his power.

The Doctor's attempts at persuading the Sea Devils to act peaceably are thwarted when Walker, a politician, leads an attack against them. Eventually Walker lets him try again, but the Sea Devils have already taken over the naval base.

The Doctor is made to assist the Master, but manages to destroy both machine and Sea Devils.

able to achieve this, giving extra drama to his work that was very much a part of his style. To avoid a technicolour appearance in his work, he would subdue many of the coloured inks and use a limited colour scheme. In the black and white work there is a clever use of shadow and in some instances he would try and put in the very least that he could and yet still convey the maximum impact.

He saw things as a film director would, imagining the potential of all he observed for use in an illustration, and he loved anything that was a bit different from the ordinary. He would see things from ground level, bird's eye view, wide angled lens, telephoto lens – he seemed to have this way of looking at subjects from about a dozen differing viewpoints instead of the normal eye level from which the average person would take a photograph. I cannot help speculating what a good combination somebody like Steven Speilberg and my father would have been and I think he would have liked to have directed films but never thought of it as anything more than just a fantasy, although he certainly had dreams which he recalled as mini-films. In the

THE MUTANTS

The cruel Marshal of Solos wants to prevent its independence from Earth—and arranges the death of the official from Earth.

Entrusted with a secret message from the Time Lords, the Doctor and Jo arrive on Solos, where the Doctor is taken prisoner. Jo, meanwhile, is led to the surface of the planet by Ky, the Solonian falsely blamed for the murder. Here, Sondergaard a doctor, is researching into the cause of the Solonians' mutation. The Doctor gets away, follows Jo and Ky, and encounters Sondergaard, but is taken prisoner again.

But the Time Lords' message indicates the location of a special crystal. Sondergaard gives this to Ky, who mutates, eventually becoming a super-being and killing the Marshal. The Solonians' mutation is an unusual form of evolution measured in hundreds of years!

Italian 'spaghetti westerns' he felt the director really used the camera to the best of his ability – extreme close-ups, and long distance shots, the use of sound and image combined which he felt was very good from a visual point of view. He was just an illustrator twenty-four hours a day ; was totally absorbed in it and regarded it as a very serious way of earning a living, becoming quite annoyed with anyone who thought to the contrary.

My father's method of tackling his work was in many ways quite bizarre. Starting with a piece of clean white CS10 line board he would sketch away very loosely in a soft pencil and in his own mind he must have been visualising the image, for there was nothing really worked out beforehand, nor any tracings that I recall. When he had this rough, soft image on the board, he would start inking in areas with a dip pen which he found very handy to use because he liked the flexibility of the nib. In this way he would build up the picture and at a particular stage it would suddenly become a wonderful piece of black and white illustration. When every single aspect of it was, in his eyes, technically finished and did not require any blurring of highlight areas, he would then apply the rotring coloured inks. He limited himself to vermillion red, ultramarine blue and yellow and these he would mix very carefully in a palette containing about sixty sections. He knew his own colour ranges and worked very, very quickly with large sable brushes, lots of blotting paper and cotton wool and would do what was almost like an incredible magic trick – an illusion – suddenly things would appear that were unbelievable. He worked at a fantastic speed and did without all the usual methods used by a good number of artists, in that they

THE THREE DOCTORS

A black hole is swallowing up the energy of the Time Lords and a Cosmic Ray Research Balloon is sent to probe. It brings back a dematerialising blob which continues to grow, trapping the Doctor and Jo in the TARDIS.

To assist the Doctor the Time Lords send for his earlier forms. The three Doctors pool their intellects and find out that Omega, a forgotten Time Lord, is imprisoned in anti-matter behind the black hole. In his misery Omega wants to change places with the Doctor, but only his mind survives. His intention is to wipe out the Universe.

The three Doctors arrange his transformation into a supernova. Omega can now channel his energy into boosting the resources of the Time Lords. The Doctors return to their own places in Time.

trace, select, try out images on a visualiser camera and then work the drawing up, transferring the work onto the board, working on top of that until finally all the pieces are in place. My father just did not use these techniques.

Working at such an astronomical speed meant that he could convey his idea straight from his brain to the actual board itself in the shortest possible time. I never saw him labour on anything – it was a 'to the point' way of illustrating that is rather hard to describe. I particularly remember him working on the 'Doctor Who and the Loch Ness Monster', the original of which I own, where Tom Baker is saying 'We're dealing with a monster that is not of ordinary flesh and blood' – there is an area of red at the back of Tom Baker's head and I recall this being flashed in – really whizzed in – it came through many years of just being an illustrator from the minute he woke up to the minute he went to bed. He hadn't any hobbies – all his interests were ones which enhanced his expertise or reputation in illustration itself.

All the work he did on *Doctor Who* was, I remember, done at this incredible pace. The deadlines were short but he seemed to be able to do things in a couple of hours. From wandering upstairs with a script in his hands and maybe a good reference photo, a few hours later a beautifully presented piece of artwork would appear. It was

THE CARNIVAL OF MONSTERS

The Doctor and Jo are miniature exhibits in a show! The TARDIS is trapped out of its time in the midst of a display of galactic creatures. This spectacle, called the Scope, is run by the enterprising showman, Vorg.

When the Doctor attempts to break out through another part of the Scope, he finds himself in a swamp inhabited by Drashigs, giant aquatic beasts. At last he escapes and returns to life size, but has to outwit Kalik and Orum who are plotting the demise of their President. They intend to release the Drashigs.

But Vorg kills the Drashigs and the Doctor connects the Scope and TARDIS together to break the time loop in which they are stuck. All the exhibits are sent back to their proper places in Time and Space.

FRONTIER IN SPACE

The TARDIS materialises with the Doctor and Jo in a spaceship from Earth. But no sooner do they arrive than the ship is under attack. The Earthmen think their attackers are Draconians, but the Doctor and Jo recognise them as Ogrons, the Daleks' slaves.

Suspected of spying for Draconia, they are despatched to the Moon where the Master rescues them, but he is trying to incite a war between Earth and Draconia. The Doctor escapes, only to be taken by the Draconians who suspect him of spying for Earth, but eventually believe his story.

Meanwhile, the Master takes Jo to the Ogrons' planet. The Doctor follows, and finds out that the whole scheme of war has been plotted by the Daleks! The plan is foiled, but the Doctor is critically injured.

an instant explosion onto the board. He would then say 'do you think I could improve it in any way ? What do you think ?' – he seemed shy about the fact of having done it, but of course there was nothing I could say or any way I would have wanted to see it changed. The work was a wonderful spontaneous statement, and that is something very rare. I have seen many illustrations by other artists that appear to have been done in a similar way but look to me unnatural and were copied techniques that did not come easily to the artists.

My father found a way of working with line, shadow and dot stipple that, while I would say it was not easy to do, he

found particularly satisfying. None of it was easy for him but it was a very natural way of working and his style evolved without being influenced by anyone else, although he admired Norman Rockwell, the American illustrator, as his work was so beautifully observed.

Working with coloured inks was a great love of my father's and he stayed with them through his entire career – I don't think he possessed anything other than these. I had various designer's paint tubes and he saw the things I did but was never tempted to use them. Inks are a very difficult medium to work with particularly on CS10 line board which is not at all sympathetic as the inks tend to dry unevenly, yet he could wash in skies or flat areas of

THE PLANET OF EVIL

The Doctor and Sarah land on Zeta Minor, the planet at the very edge of the known Universe and become entangled in a desperate nightmare. They find Professor Sorenson, the only survivor of a geological expedition from 'the planet Morestra. Other members of his team have been killed by an invisible entity which originates from a universe of anti-matter for which Zeta Minor is the gateway.

When eventually a rescue probe with the Doctor, Sarah and Sorenson on board attempts to leave the planet the situation worsens, the Professor having taken with him some anti-matter. He turns into a monster and the ship is pulled back to the planet. The Doctor succeeds in returning the material to the anti-matter universe and secures both the freedom of the ship from the planet and a cure for Professor Sorenson.

DAY OF THE DALEKS

Travelling back in time from the twenty-second century, a group of guerillas attack Sir Reginald Styles, a diplomat. They claim he is responsible for the assassinations which lead to the future war through which the Daleks take over the world. They wish to stop this happening.

The guerillas, who in their own time are under the yoke of the Daleks and their primitive servants, the Ogrons, journey back to the future. Travelling with them, the Doctor discovers that the real assassin is Shura, one of the guerillas on the mission to kill Styles.

The Doctor escapes and returns swiftly to the present day and makes everyone leave Styles' house. Shura drops a Dalekanium bomb on it, but only the Daleks and Ogrons are killed, thus preventing the future war.

35

colour and give an almost airbrushed effect. This was done so quickly with brushes, blotting paper, cotton wool and various other little tricks, it was like watching a magician, the quickness of the hand deceiving the eye. It was really quite hard to tell just what happened at times. Try and observe an artist at work and they will inevitably slow down waiting for you to go, so I used to watch my father working almost out of the corner of my eye. He had many books in his room and I used to wander in asking for so and so title, observing him while scanning the book. I was always impressed by his incredible expertise when handling the medium – it was never a problem, being totally and utterly dominated by him. The illustration would suddenly

THE ARK IN SPACE

The future inhabitants of Earth are stored in a giant space station. They have been placed in deep freeze to be kept safe until Earth, laid waste by the solar flares, can be colonised again. But the control equipment has malfunctioned and the Humans continue to remain asleep.

Carried there by the TARDIS, the Doctor finds that giant insect-like Wirrn have invaded the station and Wirrn eggs have been laid in the body of Noah in an attempt to dominate the Earth. To kill the Wirrn Noah, the commander of the Ark, blows himself and Wirrn up.

The Doctor, Sarah and Harry travel down to Earth to confirm that the planet is now suitable for the humans to return to live.

PLANET OF THE DALEKS

The Daleks escape to the planet Spiridon, where the Doctor and Jo also materialise. Unaware of the Doctor's great ability to recover from his Dalek inflicted wounds, Jo goes on her own in search of help and encounters the Thals. Friends of the Time Lords, they aim to crush the Daleks whatever the cost to themselves. Jo falls ill, but is mysteriously cured by an invisible native.

Meanwhile, the Doctor has recovered and the Thals inform him of a great army of Daleks left in suspended animation by the cold. They have forced the Spiridons to assist them since they know the secret of invisibility. When the Doctor locates the Daleks he manages to induce an ice volcano into activity so that the whole army becomes completely frozen again.

appear as though a print were developing in a darkroom.

He never did any meticulous tracing of images or photographs although he might have had a piece of tracing paper for about ten years that was roughly six by four inches and which he used over again for odds and ends! The *Radio Times* would send a photographic reference for the illustration and this was laid on the side of his drawing board and occasionally looked at, as my father liked to get the essence of the photograph and then illustrate what he felt were the most important elements. I never observed him comparing the photograph with his artwork to see if it tallied up. It was a very instantaneous technique.

My father had very definite ideas about what should and should not be done in illustration and he regarded getting it right as a very strong discipline. His originals were always scrupulously clean as he never used process white, although it would never have shown on the actual printed work. Some people who didn't know a great deal about illustration would look at the original and ask if it was a print of the real thing. I recall some friends of mine came round and my father showed some of his work to them and they were amazed that there was no retouching. One said, 'that will be the last time I ever use process white – it will teach me to be more of a technician and to avoid mistakes.'

THE GREEN DEATH

Professor Clifford Jones has founded a commune in a Welsh valley but the peaceful environment is disturbed when the giant Global Chemicals constructs and puts into production a large refinery. The Professor's fears of pollution are soon realised and UNIT is called in to investigate a death in mysterious circumstances.

Recently returned from Metebelis 3, the Doctor finds some lethal giant maggots and algae, and traces their source to waste from the refinery. Confronting the local director of Global Chemicals, he discovers that his mind is being controlled by BOSS, the giant computer behind the company.

To break the spell the Doctor uses a Blue Crystal brought back from Metebelis 3. The computer is beaten and reason prevails, preventing any more pollution. Jo marries Professor Jones and is given the Blue Crystal.

THE SEEDS OF DOOM

Two unusual seed pods are found in the Antarctic and a research station is taken over when one of the pods bursts open and proceeds to sprout. They turn out to be dreaded Krynoids, plants which signal doom to all Earthly animal life.

Harrison Chase, a mad wealthy botanist, wants to acquire the other pod and despatches two men to steal it. They manage to obtain the pod, but in the fight the giant Krynoid and the research base are destroyed.

At Chase's mansion his Krynoid soon grows, but its evilness starts to infect other plant life. The Doctor and UNIT try to prevent a disaster, but the only solution is to destroy the monster plant. RAF Phantoms bomb the Krynoid before it can disperse its seeds.

The evening was his favourite time for working and he always got up rather late in the morning mainly because he went to bed very late at night. Many evenings we spent together chatting and were surprised to suddenly hear this

SPEARHEAD FROM SPACE

The TARDIS is inoperative. The Doctor, stranded on Earth in the twentieth century, is called in to investigate a shower of meteorites which have fallen. He discovers that they are carrying Nestenes, a form of intelligence which takes over planets by imitating the indigenous life forms. Already the local factory is under the control of a Nestene called Channing.

Nestenes have a particular facility for using plastic, and Channing is producing facsimiles of government ministers to gain control of the world. He has also manufactured an army of plastic Autons which are directed by the Nestene Consciousness.

But the Doctor overpowers the Nestenes and the mission of killing by the Autons is prevented.

The Doctor stays as an adviser to UNIT until the TARDIS is operational.

TERROR OF THE ZYGONS

The mystery of the Loch Ness Monster is unravelled by the Doctor. Called to investigate strange happenings in the surrounding area, he discovers that a Zygon space-ship has been marooned at the bottom of the Loch for hundreds of years. The Zygons have created the Monster, a Skarasen. Half machine and half animal, it is attacking the North Sea oil rigs.

Since their planet has been annihilated the Zygons want to make Earth their home. They can assume the form of Humans and are gradually taking over the nearby village. The Doctor reveals their identities and the Zygon ship is destroyed. Their leader, Broton, sets out to inflict chaos on the World Energy Conference by using the Skarasen, but the Doctor foils his plans.

The Monster still lives in Loch Ness!

twittering sound outside, draw the curtains, find it was early morning and the birds were getting up !

Whilst working he used to play tapes of film music as background – he felt that this produced the right mood for creating the drama of his work, and each of his illustrations

GENESIS OF THE DALEKS

The long war between the Thals and Kaleds on the planet Skaro is nearing its end. The Doctor is sent to Skaro by the Time Lords. He must try to stop the creation of the Daleks!

To preserve the Kaleds, who have been weakened by war, one of their scientists, Davros, has invented a travel machine. But Davros is including an evil element in his invention and the machines will actually become Daleks! Led by the Doctor, the scientists rise against Davros, but he is beyond all reason. He activates the Daleks, wiping out Kaleds and Thals.

But the Doctor traps Davros and the scientist himself is eventually destroyed by the Daleks. Though the Daleks are evil, the Doctor refuses to commit genocide believing that good will eventually come from them.

had a suitable musical accompaniment to their creation. It was the combination of sounds in film themes that he enjoyed as opposed to pop or classical music.

His studio working area was jam packed with books and pieces of Africana which he was particularly interested in. He was always mad about Africa, ever since he was a boy and had many books on the continent. Sitting in a floppy directors-type chair, he would work at an angled drawing board upon which was clipped a piece of CS10 with all the rest of the desk cluttered with pens and bottles of ink and the inevitable ash tray full of cigarette ends.

Although he wasn't particularly thrilled by science fiction my father's creations in that field were ahead of their

time, as he saw things in a totally different light to other illustrators and seemed to have an almost visionary approach to what he was doing. The world gone by was his preference and when he illustrated Robin Hood or anything medieval he found the fascination of that era far more intriguing. I remember he once said that when watching science fiction films he thought they lacked drama as anything was possible which he considered a cop out. The past was infinitely more attractive to him than a seemingly dismal future with computers and gadgetry which left him unimpressed.

When he drew the *Doctor Who* front cover of the *Radio Times*, Jon Pertwee, who was portrayed with the Daleks,

saw the original piece of artwork in the *Radio Times* offices and he left a note saying 'I really thought it was a wonderful piece of work', which was passed on to my father. Bob Monkhouse is probably the biggest 'personality' collector of my father's work that I know of, and he has a room displaying Frank Bellamy artwork.

I was intrigued by the incredible number of letters my father received from people all over the world. They would write to say 'I think that the way you did so and so illustration was really quite wonderful' enclosing samples of their work which ranged from the really terrible to quite good, and he would always write back to them a very positive and encouraging letter. It didn't seem to annoy him in any way that he would be asked so many questions – I believe he regarded it as very flattering that people should write from the other side of the world perhaps not expecting a reply. But eventually they would and I hope this encouraged them to carry on.

He was probably the most consistent of illustrators and it is fascinating to realise that from his first published illustrations to the very last ones, they were all good in differing ways. The techniques changed over the years – each were good and appropriate to the story, magazine or the newspaper in which they appeared. It was an amazing achievement, I think, not turning in a bad illustration over all those years. In an embarrassed way he used to say that the editor who had received his latest artwork was, to use his favourite term, 'over the moon by it', almost as if it surprised him. To produce pictures that had this incredible power and consistency over all those years, whatever the subject, turning it out all the time, fifty-two weeks a year with almost no holidays, I find fascinating and intriguing to look back upon.

David Bellamy.

TIMEVIEWED

FRANK BELLAMY: THE DOCTOR WHO ILLUSTRATIONS

COLONY IN SPACE: 10/4/71
A two and a half page picture strip illustrating part of episode one's storyline. Two of the pages in full colour. An additional line drawing accompanied the programme page.

THE DAEMONS: 2/5/71 and 29/12/71
Two line illustrations, the second for the 'omnibus' re-run.

DAY OF THE DALEKS: 1/1/72
Full colour cover illustration.

THE CURSE OF PELADON: 1972
This story sees Bellamy contributing for the first time (four) small portrait illustrations to accompany the cast list programme pages. This continued up to and including 'The Green Death'.

THE SEA DEVILS: 1972
Five small illustrations and in addition a large montage illustrating the 'omnibus' re-run 27/12/85.

THE MUTANTS: 1972
Six small illustrations

THE THREE DOCTORS: 1973
Three small illustrations

THE CARNIVAL OF MONSTERS: 1973
Three small illustrations

FRONTIER IN SPACE: 1973
Six small illustrations

PLANET OF THE DALEKS: 1973
Six small illustrations

THE GREEN DEATH: 1973
Six small illustrations

THE ARK IN SPACE: 25/1/75
A large landscape illustration

TERROR OF THE ZYGONS: 30/8/75
A large full colour illustration for a feature page plus a large line drawing to accompany the programme page.

GENESIS OF THE DALEKS: 27/12/75
A large line drawing in strip form to promote the first re-run of this story.

54

THE SEEDS OF DOOM: 31/1/76
One medium size line illustration.

THE PLANET OF EVIL: 5/7/76
Frank Bellamy's last Doctor Who piece for the Radio Times – a large landscape illustration promoting the consecutive evening re-runs of the story.

SPEARHEAD FROM SPACE
Bellamy drew one small line drawing for a re-run of this particular story.

BBC EXHIBITIONS
An illustration commissioned for use on promotional posters and leaflets for the Blackpool exhibition between 1975 and 1977.

Where a detailed date is given, this refers to the issue of the Radio Times.

The Publishers would be glad to hear from anyone who owns or knows of the whereabouts of any of Frank Bellamy's original artwork, whether for Doctor Who or any other subject matter, with a view to keeping an archival record of his work and possible future publication. All sources of information received will be kept confidential.

THE WRITERS

Spearhead from Space: Robert Holmes
Colony in Space: Malcolm Hulke
The Daemons: Guy Leopold
The Day of the Daleks: Louis Marks
The Curse of Peladon: Brian Hayles
The Sea Devils: Malcolm Hulke
The Mutants: Bob Baker, Dave Martin
The Three Doctors: Bob Baker, Dave Martin
Carnival of Monsters: Robert Holmes
Frontier in Space: Malcolm Hulke
Planet of the Daleks: Terry Nation
The Green Death: Robert Sloman
The Ark in Space: Robert Holmes
Genesis of the Daleks: Terry Nation
Terror of the Zygons: Robert Banks Stewart
Planet of Evil: Louis Marks
The Seeds of Doom: Robert Banks Stewart

Who Dares Publishing announce the start of an exciting new publishing list with an emphasis on illustrative content and first class design and production.

THE MAN WHO DREW TOMORROW

An illustrated account of the life and work of FRANK HAMPSON, how he co-created EAGLE, Britain's most famous comic in 1950, created, wrote and drew the legendary DAN DARE, Pilot of the Future strip and went on to be voted by an International Jury of his peers in 1975 the best post-war writer and artist of strip cartoons. Fully illustrated, using original artwork, sketches from Hampson's notebooks and studio photos. This book shows for the first time how Hampson ran The Dan Dare Studio and anticipated Starwars in the degree of research and preparation he put into the adventures of his space hero.

Who Dares produces a wide range of DOCTOR WHO merchandise featuring the outstanding artwork of Andrew Skilleter, internationally known for his visual interpretations of the worlds of Doctor Who. This established imprint is recognised for its high standard of design and print.

THE CALENDAR

Each year Who Dares produces a full colour calendar featuring paintings on the theme of Doctor Who by Andrew Skilleter, beautifully presented and produced. A World Exclusive for Who Dares.

THE BOOKMARKS & ARTCARDS

Two ranges in full colour featuring the Doctors and characters from the series. Many of the Bookmarks are blockfoiled in silver or gold and both have writing space on the reverse.

THE POSTER PRINTS

A full colour range featuring paintings by Andrew Skilleter of the Doctors and his adversaries. Encapsulated in laminate film for lasting protection.

If you have any difficulty in obtaining any of these items please write to:

United Kingdom: Who Dares Publishing,
3 Durrant Road
Bournemouth Dorset
BH2 6NE
United States: Lyle Stuart Inc.
120 Enterprise Avenue
Secaucus
New Jersey 07094
Australia: ABC Enterprises
Box 9994 GPO Sidney 2001

Please note: Not all items listed are available from the above United States or Australian addresses.